INSIDE

MANEUVERS

Mikal Ali

Copyright © 2020 Mikal Ali.

All rights reserved. No part of this publication may be reproduced, distributed, or transmitted in any form or by any means, including photocopying, recording, or other electronic or mechanical methods, without the prior written permission of the publisher, except in the case of brief quotations embodied in critical reviews and certain other noncommercial uses permitted by copyright law. To maintain the anonymity of the individuals mentioned, I have changed their names.

First paperback edition May 2020

ISBN: 9798643455851

Imprint: Independently published

Book Cover Designer: Mikal Ali

THE INTRODUCTION

As Jay-Z, one of my favorite rappers quoted in his immortal words, "We ain't even posed to be here, but since we here, it's only right that we be fed." on his *Niggas in Paris* hit. His words struck me hard, I interpreted it and applied it to my own struggle. I spent twelve years in Georgia's prison system, and like Jay, I felt like I wasn't supposed to be there, but since I was, I decided to devote myself to making it profitable and productive—being fed. So, in this body of work, I've recorded my experiences in the system. Some of them being my own, and others being stories of those whom I've met along the way and how they managed to "catch".

In a position of powerlessness, many convicts have discovered the subtle ability to manipulate officers, use their creativity, charm, persuasion, and other elements to develop a reality of power and control among the powerless. They have not only seduced women into sex and romantic relationships, but have also made hundreds of thousands of dollars by getting them to bring contraband; from phones to drugs into the prisons.

Essentially, everything is a science, and by it being a science there's a way to learn the science, apply the principles, and see the results that will inevitably come from proper application of the laws. I call this a science because it has been tried, tested, and experimented. We know what always works, what can work, and what never works at all.

Many different authors have written books on this subject, and they are in-depth works that lay down a wide range of information on this topic. But no one has done anything that can be applied directly to prison. In prison, the playing field is slightly different. Women who aren't beauties on the street, are beauties in prison, because hard up convicts blow their heads up giving them the illusion that they're desirable. Several other factors bring a slight difference to the psychological makeup of women who work in prisons. These are some of the details that I go into in this book.

Seduction is an art form, and was originally developed centuries ago by women. From the beginning of time power was wielded strictly by men. By using violence and force, men have raged wars for the hunger of power. Countries were solidified, and nations were forged by the brute force of man's greed and ambition. Under these conditions women were the victims during this dynamic. They had no weapons at their disposal, except one, which was man's weakness for sex. Great women throughout history, with ingenuity and cleverness, used this powerful weapon to elevate them to heights of power that no man could imagine. They realized the powerful truth, that essentially, pussy runs the world!

These women, from Cleopatra, Helen of Troy, and more modern figures such as Madonna, Jennifer Lopez, and Kim Kardashian, as well as countless others, invented seduction. Usually, they would get a man's attention with an alluring appearance, using makeup and other sexual fashions. They would arouse men's imaginations by not revealing too much of their bodies, but just enough to have men's minds running wild. With the way they played the game, they did more than stimulate the desire for sex, they created an illusion that the man was actually getting a chance to have a fantasy figure. After they captured the victims' minds by using exotic lures, they would whisk them away from their daily routines, and send them into a fantasy world of luxury and pleasure.

Men would be hooked and fall in love with these sensual pleasures. Then, at the proper time, the woman would turn cold, just when their victims wanted more, they would take away their delights, leaving them confused. Now the men would be in hot pursuit, doing anything to win back the joy and bliss that they had experienced. Now the dynamic was suddenly switched. Men with great power and control, were now emotional slaves to these women who had played them.

These great women now had a sophisticated art at their hands, the ultimate form of power and persuasion. They worked the mind first, their power was not in the traditional physical sense, it was psychological. Not forceful, but clever and subtle. The science of seduction was viewed by its female originators as the feminine version of warfare, because with it, not only did they seduce men in power, but they took over whole empires and countries with its tactics.

For them, it was more than just playing with an individual man and his desires, it was much larger than that. It was a means by which they could conquer the world. Today, in our smaller reality behind these walls, we can use these same tactics to control our environments, gain power, and earn a lot of money. Remember, its bigger than this crush you have on this chick, this is your way to elevate your status to one of power.

In the beginning, men didn't concern themselves with the science of seduction, it was a woman's game. But that all changed near the seventeenth century when men began to interest themselves in breaking down young women's resistance to sex, thus the use of seduction was implored.

Many legendary men began to use these tactics, first developed by women, to their advantage. They learned how to attract with their appearance. They learned to switch from hot to cold at appropriate times. And they also innovated the game in ways that women couldn't, mainly by using seductive language, for they had learned a woman's weakness for flowery speech.

Today, in the prison environment, seduction is more important than ever, for the act of force will gain you nothing but extra time when trying to use it on the COs. Also, seduction can be powerful when trying to influence gangs and other organizations, in this way it becomes a major social tool. You can use some of the same tactics to sway leaders of organizations and have the whole gang under your influcnce. I've seen many nonaffiliated convicts manipulate organizations and end up earning money for everyone involved and have them as an army on their side as well, without ever actually joining the gang.

My main aim in this book is the women in the prison system that are overly susceptible to falling in love with a convict. I construct a game plan to get into the minds of these targets and give you a better chance at them falling in love with you. Once you get them to surrender, they'll be open to anything you suggest. This book is the science of making people fall in love. As a master of this art it is pivotal to take your time, never rush into anything. Besides, being in prison you have nothing but time on your side.

As I mentioned earlier, our objective is bigger than this one officer whom you have entranced in your manipulations. It is the power that is gained after you have played the game how it is supposed to be played. Once you wield this power and hold on to it by making the right moves, you'll be able to control your confined environment and open doors that you could not imagine before.

Anyone can develop the traits that lead to this kind of power. It has very little to do with looks or physical prowess, these are only tools that some people have. Everyone has something seductive about them. These natural traits are what you are to identify within yourself and cultivate them for your advantage. Each seductive type that I note in this book are different in their own ways, but the same in the fact that women are easily allured by these character types. Remember, this is a mental game, not physical.

Part of your task is to make the target have a pleasurable experience when you come around. This will make them yearn to be around you and enjoy your presence. It is important that you view all of your interactions as a potential seduction. In this way. your charm is always turned on, and you gain adequate practice from encounters that don't really seem to matter. Keep your personality on high at all times, sharing your light with everyone.

To master the science of the catch, you should view people as a fortress whose thick armored walls you are trying to penetrate. The conscious mind is the gate, the first barrier that you must learn to bypass. Once you've gotten into their heads, the rest is easy. You must strategize, never leaving anything to chance, plan out all run ins with your target, what you'll say, your gestures and all.

Learn to see things from your target's point of view. Find out what they're into, their weaknesses, and tailor your pursuit according to that. Get out of your own skin, never be self-absorbed, this shows insecurity and is anti-seductive. Whatever your insecurities, ignore them as if you have none, instead focus on your target's insecurities, this is how you can get under their skin.

Stop viewing women as beautiful butterflies that you fantasize about, and how valuable they seem to you. Learn to start seeing yourself as the prize and make it a thrill for them to be in your presence. Become a flame that attracts all. Become a joy to be around, add value to the conversations, wherever you find them. People are always in want of pleasure, make yourself the one that delivers it to them. A person who offers pleasure and excitement is not easily resisted. Make them overwhelmed by your character. Eventually you'll find that your target will come to you, seeking you out.

Life, especially life in prison, is a movie. Officers and convicts alike put on roles, and mask to hide who they really are. How many times have you run into guys who lie about their past and what they've done? How many people have you known who transfer to different facilities and change their nicknames? Or they acted this way here, but act totally different now? Officers are the same way. Essentially, we're all human, and human behavior is the same. So, treat your situation as a movie and approach it with that view in mind. This officer is probably not what she seems on the surface. This is especially true when you run into officers that seem really strict or mean. More than likely they act differently at home. It's your job to probe into the mind of the real person behind the mask.

You'll discover that most officers that work in prison are brutally unhappy, they live a life as constricted or even more so than yours as a convict. You on the other hand, can paint an image of whatever you want, and present it to your target. Sometimes it's good to be yourself, but if your true self is not conducive to your select target, then feel free to put on another mask. In fact, people secretly love a heightened persona, a dreamlike figure, even if they know it's too good to be true. They have a need to believe, a want to believe that will keep them clinging to you. Why do you think people love movies anyway? They know the characters aren't real, but for that two-hour period they were taken away from the harsh reality of their drab lives, even if only temporarily.

Understand, also, there is nothing to be ashamed of when dealing with manipulation. In most cases you'll be doing your victims a favor. They were secretly yearning for the adventure that you provided. The excitement of living a double life, it was as if you two were playing out parts in your own movie. It's up to you to play by the rules and not get them caught up, but if played correctly, you'll both gain financially and have a fun, stimulating experience.

This book is to help you hone your natural skills at attraction, persuasion and influence. I want to provide power to the powerless. There are two things you must learn before you try your hand at seduction. First, learn who you are, and what is attractive about you. I don't care how ugly, or lame you may think you are, everyone has something that will work in their favor, sometimes you just have to further develop it. Two, learn everything you can about your target, study them, and find out the best way to get into their heads. All of these officers are searching for something.

Find out what that 'something' is and be the one who can provide it—or at least create the illusion that you can. Both of these steps are critical. You have to learn what makes you attractive and use it thoroughly, and you have to learn what makes your target tick. Like I've mentioned above, both of these steps are essential to a successful seduction; you can't have one without the other. If you approach your game armed with only your character, then she may like you, but you're not providing what she really wants, you'll only get so far, especially if she's in a relationship like most officers are. If you only pay attention to what she wants, then she'll be interested in what you offer, but may not want to deal with your character. You never want to limit your chances, leave nothing to chance. Everything is calculated, this is a science.

I have broken this book down into three parts. The first part, I go into the different types of convicts that I am aware of. All of them are characters that I've experienced for myself, by meeting different people of catch type and trying my own endeavors. In twelve years I have saw everything that a Georgia prison had to offer—things may run slightly differently in your state, but still, human nature will essentially be the same.

I have covered everything I could think of, but as I've said, this is my experience, so I wouldn't be surprised if some people have more information to provide. Read each of these types and identify which one closely resembles yourself. It is possible that more than one fits you, but try to embody the one that predominates. In each type, I describe the traits, and then I go into a specific person who I've met, and talked with. Those individuals shared their game, experiences, and knowledge with me. I've had the privilege to sit and learn directly from these powerful people, the very knowledge I now share with you. In each story, pay attention to the details, and study the ways in which they utilized their character traits. I have studied, crashed and burned and bled for you so that my failed attempts and successes can be a guide to your success.

Trust me, I've been under private investigation for personal dealings on numerous occasions. I've gotten many DRs and write ups and other disciplinary infractions for doing things that I shouldn't have done when approaching different officers. All of the material I have collected for this book has been tried and tested. It is sure to work if you apply the knowledge and apply yourself correctly. I've devoted my prison sentence to the study of this science. I have left nothing out, this includes the good, the bad, and the ugly of how to catch an officer.

In section two, I briefly describe the different types of victims, who I call targets. This is a basic outline of the type of people who typically work in prisons. You also have some who I didn't mention, those who are satisfied with their careers and plan on moving up the ladder, these are nearly impossible to catch, but anything's possible. With each type I have included some tale tell signs to let you know how to categorize them, and I've laid out a basic strategy to approach them.

In the final and third section of this book, I explain the various ways to approach your target. Some are more in depth than others, depending on how much experience I have with the particular ones. These strategies can be used to trick your target or get into their heads easily. One or two are simply strong arming your way into getting them to move, but these aren't really encouraged by me. I like the finesse approach, not the forceful guerilla style, but they work.

This book is better used as a reference book. It would be difficult for you to read once and be able to use its information, so I advise you purchase a copy of your own so that you can study it thoroughly and be able to refer back to some of its chapters when you need to. This can be a valuable tool that can elevate you on both a financial and social level.

Remember the reason why you're venturing into this world, because it is a world of its own, and keep that intention in mind.

Don't get discouraged if you fail in your first few attempts after reading this book. You may fail a few times before you get it right. Each failure should be viewed as a necessary stepping stone to your inevitable mastery. Simply reading and studying this book won't make you a professional at the game, you have to get out there, crash and burn a few times before you get the hang of what you're doing. This book is a guide, it won't make the journey for you, you have to take that trip. So, with that being said, I hope you find success in your endeavors. I hope you gain the financial potential that lies behind these prison walls. I hope his book awakens the powerful individual that rest within you and I hope that you maintain your strength well beyond these walls. Much success to you!

PART ONE
THE SEDUCTIVE TYPES

Everyone has the power to attract within them. We possess something about us that can be used in seduction, no matter how deeply buried it may be. Unfortunately, most of us are not aware of these qualities and we think that only a select few are born with this advantage. Truth is, all we have to do is become aware of our potential, and understand what it is about ourselves that naturally draws people to us, and further cultivate these traits. Me personally, I believe that any man at any time can seduce any woman. No matter how ugly he may be, or how fine she may be, he has a chance. However slim that chance may be varies, but he still has a chance. With the right words, the right approach, he can get her. You'll soon learn that it's not physical looks when it comes to women, men are into looks, women are into how you make them feel. Surely you've met or seen guys with beautiful women, but they were a toad. These relationships happen all the time. And it's not about money either.

Effective seduction rarely starts with an obvious move or conversation. This usually instills suspicion in your targets. In prison, the officers are briefed on what to look for when they're approached by convicts, so this training has already placed their guards extremely high against you trying to seduce them. Effective seduction starts with your character, your capability to exude a quality that stirs emotions in others that they can't contain.

Overwhelmed by your character, your victims will fail to notice any mind games you play and leading them will be easy. I have included ten seducer types. These are the types of characters that I have watched get officers in prison. Each type has a unique aspect that they use to catch what they want.

The Flashy Guy has an appeal to the eyes of his victims, he looks like money, rather or not he actually possesses it. Women are attracted to flashy things, so he becomes like the rainbow that leads his victims to the pot of gold, that's usually an illusion.

The Stand-Up Guy is a real man, a natural leader. He's honest and sticks to his word. He's confident and possesses many other masculine traits that women are naturally attracted to. Women are designed to follow men, so it comes quite easily for a Stand-Up Guy to maneuver.

The Pretty Boy puts a lot of work into his appearance, sometimes he even has a touch of femininity that women find familiar. His appearance is attractive, which he uses to lure women in.

The Funny Guy is a natural charmer. He brings out the repressed childish nature in people and takes them away from the drudgery of their everyday life.

The Homo gets into female officer's head very easily, especially if they're the feminine type of homosexual. They give them something they can relate to and are easy to talk to. Also, women guards are lowered because they think that the homosexual does not want sex from them.

The Money Man is quite obvious why he can catch. All women love money and men who have it.

The Intellectual appeals to those women who are smart themselves and can't get stimulating conversations from anyone.

These and many more have special qualities that attract women. Find out which one you are, and work on strengthening these traits. This will be the key to your power. There is no point in going halfway with your seduction type, once you discover who you are, go all the way and fully envelop yourself in it. Only then will people really notice it within you, and the confidence you'll exude from it. Once you've mastered one type, you may choose to take on another, depending on what may be more appealing to your victim.

Often, you'll notice that you already possess a mixture of the types already. Study these types, and then continue to embark on your journey to seductive mastery.

THE FLASHY GUY

Seduction is a type of language that speaks to the subconscious mind. The reasons why this is necessary, is because we are bombarded on a daily basis by different elements competing for our attention. Everything is obvious and highly manipulative, we are rarely deceived by this. This keeps us on high alert, and overly suspicious of everything.

By trying to appeal to a person's conscious mind by being direct with what we want, is often met with rejection. You become another element that gets ignored. Although a lot of people assume that it's better to be direct and say exactly what you want from the jump, these people are mistaken. How are you gonna look stepping to a female officer, talking about how much you like her and you want her to bring you some dope and phones? Your ass is going to the hole! So don't be tricked by the assumptions of those "straight up" types, that's just foolish.

In order to get to the subconscious, one must learn how to insinuate what you want. In this way your approach will often go unnoticed —planting a seed that sprouts an idea in the targets mind days later. The most powerful speech of the subconscious is the dream. Dreams are so obsessive because they mix reality with fiction. They mix real people or situations we're familiar with, with farfetched elements that are usually pleasantly irrational. If dreams were all real, it wouldn't be interesting. Yet if it was all fake, we would feel detached from it. The mixture of the strange and familiar are what keeps us allured. This is the magic of the Flashy Guy, his flashiness is an illusion really, while he himself is what's familiar as a normal guy.

These types can have an almost obsessive effect on women. They seduce them and make them want to possess them. Their larger than life persona makes them come off as untouchable, or unapproachable. This element to their personality makes women want them even more, for women always tend to love what they can't have.

25

Most people are excessively mundane, they have a normal appearance, especially in prison. But the one with the boldness to stand out from the crowd, who isn't afraid to shake things up a bit, has an unlimited power at his hands. The fact that they stand out, their target has no choice but to notice them, filling their minds with their image.

One of the most effective Flashy Guys that I've ran across was a Blood member who called himself Rich. When he first came into my dorm I couldn't help but notice him. Not in a gay way, but he just stood out. He was loud and obnoxious, and he always wore some type of accessory to his clothing that stood out: different colored shoe strings, necklaces made out of wood, different designs sewed into his hats and such. He also wore a lot of jewelry, which is quite rare in prison, gold chains that hung to his waist; big flashy watches that glistened in the sun, and flashy eyewear.

He was far from the type of person I would normally associate myself with, but he apparently saw something in me. Soon after his arrival he would strike up general conversations with me out the blue, as if we'd known each other from the past. Interestingly enough, we became friends, which was highly unlikely. Rich was much more than I thought he was, more intellectual than I had originally imagined, and our background turned out to be similar since we lived in some of the same areas.

I quickly noticed that he had a good way that he interacted with women, so that was intriguing in itself, especially considering the fact that he was not handsome at all. He was very dark in complexion, his teeth were crooked, and he had a lazy eye that would often drift to the side, but women always seemed fascinated by his character. He had good energy that made you want to be around him, and he was extremely comfortable and confident in his own skin.

I'd observe him as he would approach new officers that he'd never met before. He'd come up to them like he'd known them for years. He would get loud, yelling at the top of his lungs, "Wassup Boy!" with his arms outstretched. But this was his approach to the officers, as if they were long lost friends. The woman would be taken aback, but would quickly be engaging him and laughing with him. Days later she would be in the dorm searching for him.

He schooled me on some things while we were together. He told me to be the flame that stood out and attracted all the women. I didn't fully understand his concept at first until he broke it down to me. Basically, women loved men who could take charge of a social setting without dominating it, versus those who just sit among the group and not say much at all, just soaking up the energy. He told me about adding value. Adding value is when you bring something interesting to the table, crack some humorous jokes, tell some funny stories, and have people engaged and into what you're saying.

I'd interact with women along with him sometimes just to pick up on his energy, the way he carried himself and all, the tone of his voice, his cadence. His conversations were basic enough, nothing heavy at all. He'd discuss recent or classic movies, standup comedians, new songs, and things like that. All with a playful fun undertone to the whole conversation.

He'd also wear conversation pieces, an accessory that was sure to raise questions. He'd explain how a bracelet was made or how he'd gotten this or that. He'd mention things that he'd gotten smuggled in and see what effect that would have on his target. It's good to throw little baits out there and see if your target will bite, but you have to make them subtle as possible and pay close attention to the change in their body language. He'd explain his goals of being a clothes designer and go into that world. His enthusiasm was contagious, and women would hang on his every word.

He had his own phone, so he'd get the phone numbers of nearly every girl he'd talk to and they'd spend long hours talking through the nights. While I was in the dorm with him he had convinced two female officers to bring him stuff, cell phones, drugs, whatever he wanted. He earned a lot of money throughout the time I spent with him, and I always admired the charismatic way in which he dealt with people. He was a natural.

BACKFIRE

Although Flashy Guys get a lot of women by standing out from the crowd and being different, they often get caught up and get their officers knocked off. Their flashy style gets more than just females attention, everyone tends to keep an eye on them. They also tend to have an entourage of people who love to hang with them. These people tend to be in their business, and know too much of what the flashy guys have going on. As the saying goes in prison, "If anyone knows your business, everyone does." So to play this role, you have to be extremely smart on how you maneuver. Remember to keep your business to yourself, and trust no one.

THE STAND-UP GUY

It's rare to find a woman that does not love a well-rounded man. Men are naturally the leaders and caretakers of women, so it's only natural for a woman to follow and trust a real man. One of the main tricks with seduction in prison is to build a comfort level with the woman. The Stand-Up Guy has a boss demeanor. His facial expression is serious, and he talks and walks with purpose. He is a great speaker and can get his point across, though he rarely speaks when it's not necessary. It's rare to catch them unproductive or just "kicking it", they're always on a mission and working on something. Their conversations have productive purpose, nothing frivolous at all.

This type has a charismatic energy which can be easily seductive. He can make women fall in love and lead her wherever he pleases. He has a way of making people want to impress him. Like most of the types, he stands out, but in a different way. While the Flashy Guy uses items and his appearance to stand out, the Stand-Up Guy has a natural disposition that makes him stand out. It's like he has a glow that shines through him that's almost impossible to miss. He has to have a purpose in life, and a strong belief in his purpose. His confidence is felt by everyone. But what's important is that a true Stand-Up Guy makes it appear effortless.

This type is usually pretty smart and calculating. They're leaders, and everyone tends to look up to them. Whatever they're a part of, they do it to the fullest. If they're Muslim, or religious, they envelop themselves in it and are highly devoted to it. If they're in a gang, they stand upon the truth in it, and teach those under them the right ways to practice that lifestyle.

To be this type you must naturally possess an extraordinary quality in your character. You must be truthful and honest, and filled with integrity, standing by the words you speak. This gives your personality a magnetic force that becomes the source of your power. You must speak to your target with a purpose, paint a vision for them and let them see it in their minds. You must speak in a way that creates emotion within you, which will arouse the same feelings within them. There has to be a spark in your eye, as if you're possessed by the spirit of your cause.

These guys uphold their beliefs and they don't compromise for anyone or anything! Although this type is difficult for women to detect in prison (hence why most women fall for fake guys so often) when they do detect it, they have no choice but to be attracted to him. Most Stand-Up Guys tend to be the leaders, or lone wolves, but not all leaders and lone wolves are Stand-Up Guys! The Stand-Up Guy is a rare breed, but his character always ensures success in whatever he endeavors in. Usually, the Stand-Up Guy will go unnoticed by young bombshell girls, who often fall for the fake flashy guys, or the funny guys. The few real women who have a little sense, and are more mature, will always spot a standup guy. His demeanor and his quiet strength will always stand out to the woman who knows how to look for it.

The best strategy for this type is to just fall back and be him, the right woman will let it be known when she's choosing. Usually her advances will be subtle, going out of her way to correct him, just to say something to him, or putting extra wiggle in her hips when she walks by him.

Thus, the Stand-Up Guy must be very observant and know how to read the subtle signs that women who want him will put out. When he notices who's choosing, he has to maneuver very carefully too, because a Stand-Up Guy has the highest success rate. So it's best for him to show his interest subtly as well, with small remarks, only saying hello when he sees her, then adding a little more as he goes each time he sees her. In any seduction, you never want to come on too strong, or take it too fast, or blatantly reveal your intentions.

One of the best Stand-Up Guys that I met, other than myself, was one of my Muslim brothers. His name was Ibrahim. I'd only known him for a year before he went home, but during that time he had managed to catch four officers.

Ibrahim transferred to my prison one summer. He had gotten shipped to my prison because of a conflict where he had stabbed six Blood members during a dispute over a phone. I had heard his story before I met him, so I had an image of what to expect, but I was surprised when I met him. He was in no way how I'd pictured him. He was a skinny guy, average height, light complexion, and wore his hair in a fade with curls at the top. He wore his T-shirt tucked, though he didn't have to, and his pants on his waist. He wore a low-key pair of Cartier frames, not like the wood grain design that most people wear. At first glance he would come off as a pretty boy.

He looked like a college kid, and nothing like the gangster who had ran through a group of Bloods, almost single handedly. When I spoke to him, his voice was low and smooth, but not very deep, and he kept strong eye contact. He didn't speak about the incident with the Bloods that day, nor did I bring it up even though I'd wanted details. His main concern was the condition of the camp, how the Muslims were, and how the women were. I gave him a thorough run down.

It didn't take long for him to get established at the camp. He had money saved, so he was able to purchase a phone within his first week, they ran about $800 at that time. Every conversation I held with him was productive, we never had frivolous talks. He had been down for eleven years and was about to max out on twelve and go home, so he was eager to earn as much money as possible. By this time, he had saved over $100,000. He would often discuss his strategies with women, and I was always willing to soak up as much game as I could.

One of the best forms of advice he gave me when I'd asked him about catching officers, his exact words were, "Just be Muslim. Just be Muslim."

What he was telling me was, be a Stand-Up Guy! In other words, no matter what you do, do it to the fullest, and don't bend or compromise your integrity. These few words, filled with wisdom, said so much. It said that women are attracted to powerful men, and power comes to men who stand on their beliefs. Men who control themselves can control anything.

He also told me not to be seen with too many people, and watch the company I kept, cause women often judged you by the ones you hung with. He told me whenever my target worked the dorm, never let her see me too often, stay in my room all day, only coming out for good reasons, showers and such. But never just hang out in the day room for no reason. Women love exclusivity. They want things no one else has, or only an exclusive few, this makes things more valuable. If you're not seen much, this creates the illusion that you have something going on, you're busy with something instead of hanging out.

Most guys don't understand this concept. They wish to be seen and noticed by women and end up overexposing themselves. They're eager to impress, dying for attention. Stand-Up Guys never do this. They couldn't care less about a woman's attention, it's she who needs to gain his attention and impress him. They will walk right past a sexy woman and never look her way.

By you staying out of sight, being in the room, you'll make her wonder what you've got going on, and you'll make yourself appear mysterious, interesting, and different from everyone else. This is a powerful technique. By you not paying her any attention, she'll wonder why, and in turn will make her want to get your attention.

As I mentioned earlier, he had dealt with four women during the year that I'd known him, that was more than anyone I'd known. What's more important to note here as well, is that none of them ever got caught up or fired. They all reached their goals, did everything he told them to, and quit after they made a lot of money.

He was even having a sexual relationship with one of them. By this time, he was scheduled to go home in a couple of months. I was the only one in the dorm who he had informed about what was going on with them, which is actually a violation: never tell anyone, but I was like his student so he bent the rule a bit for my education.

Every night she would bring cases of cigarettes worth thousands of dollars. Georgia prisons don't allow them so they're highly valued. He never sold anything in the dorm. He had about five people spread throughout the prison who would buy the whole pack in bulk, so his packs were presold before he even got them. By doing this, no one had a clue what he had going on, to everyone else he wasn't involved with anything.

He got reckless within his last couple weeks. His girl would sneak to his room every night, so they could have sex. Now it was me giving him advice and telling him not to be so careless, someone was surely going to rat him out. He didn't care, he was on top, getting money, and on his way home. The inevitable happened in his last week, he was caught sexing his girl. But it didn't matter, he still went home in time with well over $100,000.

THE BACKFIRE

Although this is one of the best forms of character to take on and adapt yourself, it does have a couple potential setbacks. The main one is that most of the officers that you'll find that work in prisons have never really dealt with real men, or Stand-Up Guys, so they will look rather foreign to them. As the saying goes, "Real recognizes Real", well that's true, so most of them will not recognize you when they come in contact with you. Some of them will feel intimidated by you and take you as a threat, and others will just not register you on their radar at all. This will be the problem that you'll run into the most often. You'll find that most of the young country girls who work at prisons are young and naive, and fresh out of highschool, so they are more inclined to young guys that are flashy, or funny, and carry themselves in loud and obnoxious ways, this is more in their league. But I wouldn't change up my swag to appease them, sometimes you'll just have to be patient because there are plenty of women that will recognize your worth, and work with you/ You've got nothing but time anyway.

THE FUNNY GUY

As most males already know very well, the main key to getting a girl is to make her laugh. Get her to smiling and half the work is done. But not only women, almost everyone enjoys a person with a sense of humor, because they make people comfortable, but the psyche of the Funny Guy goes deeper than just laughs.

The Funny Guy has a realness about him. He's natural and is not afraid to be himself. They oflen have a childish demeanor to them, but this is actually a good tactic. Why is being childish so seductive? Mainly because anything that comes off as natural has a heavy effect on us. These days we're surrounded by a lot of artificial and manufactured stuff, that something sudden and unexplainable excites us. Most people try too hard to please, but the Funny Guy has a natural pleasantness about him that seems effortless.

Another reason why childishness is alluring, is because it reminds people of a time that they can no longer live in the golden

43

years of childhood. Since adult life is full of responsibilities and burdens, childhood appears more carefree and peaceful even though it contains its own elements of limitations and hardships. When we come in contact with a funny, childlike individual, we subconsciously feel a nostalgic yearning for those golden years. In the presence of these types, they temporarily take us back in time, and grant us these feelings, if only for a few moments. This has an addictive effect, and so we love to be around them.

The Funny Guy is the type who is not just full of humor, but who is able to hold on to his childish traits despite the constant beatings of adulthood. Of course, this type is not exactly like a child, that would have a reverse effect. But it is the spirit that he has held on to. He often is very aware of his seductive abilities and uses them accordingly.

This is the key to this type, because they use their strength purposefully, you too can do the same. There are still remnants of that long-lost child trying to be let free. You must learn to let go of your inhibitions to a degree, there is nothing less seductive than having restraints and hesitation. Meditate on the spirit you once had and step back into it. Remember who you were before adulthood removed all of your innocence.

An example of the Funny Guy is a cat I met named Rondo. Not only was he crazy and kept everyone laughing, but he was tiny, standing at a mere 5'3" and 100 or so pounds — he had a childish look. He was a natural comedian. It was never usually what he said, but the way he said it; it was his animation and facial expressions.

He would treat all the female officers the same, rather they were ugly or not, he would joke with them, tease them, and tell them hilarious stories about his prison experiences. At first impression he was harmless. He wasn't attractive per se, so the women would have their guard down and didn't feel threatened by him, so he could easily maneuver how he wanted during his conversations with them.

After so many encounters with them they would become overly comfortable with him. Soon their innocent discourses would evolve into more mature content, then eventually into heavily detailed sexual references. Then before his victims even realized what had happened, he had gotten in their heads, and they had fallen in love with him.

When they realized that this childlike character who looked like a little boy was actually a grown man, it was too late for them to put up fences of resistance. I know of him having dealt with two officers and a counselor while we were at the same prison. His harmless conversations would always grow into the woman wanting to help this 'child', and when he sensed he had gotten them to that point, he'd hit them with the, *"Im trying to get money for a lawyer"* routine. At that point, the woman was in love with him, and was more than willing to help him get out of his situation.

This is one good example of the Funny Guy that I've personally encountered, although I've known several. Some were experts at the approach, and others didn't know how to work it fully yet. Some would get the girls to give them their numbers to call them, but could never reach the goal of getting them to bring anything, or even to fuck. But this type is very powerful if used correctly, it's one of the best types, every woman loves to laugh and loves the one who makes them laugh.

THE BACKFIRE

This type has a strong tendency to make women not want to take them seriously when it comes to handling business. Officers may kick it and hangout with you to pass their time because you're fun, but they usually won't want to risk their livelihoods by trusting you to take care of business. Sometimes these types will get phone numbers or exchange notes with officers, and maybe even get a girlfriend, but sometimes that's only as far as they go. So, learned to use this kind of persona to get you in the door with a target, and once you're in there, you have to show her a more serious side to your character. Assure her in subtle ways that you can handle making money in prison.

THE INTELLECTUAL

Women are intrigued by men who are smart. Intelligence is highly seductive. Several college girls have fallen madly in love with their professors, its common. Being that these types are thinkers, they often maneuver well throughout prison facilities.

Truthfully it isn't as effective as some of the others, because in most prisons, there aren't many highly intelligent COs, not to sound offensive, but that's just how it is. But women love smart guys, most of the time, but he has to gauge his intellect to the victim's level, and make sure he stays within her boundaries and doesn't say too many things that go over her head. If he comes off as too smart, he runs the risk of running her off by making her feel intellectually inferior. So it is wise for him to hit the target with small bits of his wisdom, expound on some topics and show her he is smart, but not to drown her in it, unless it is clear that she's also an intellectual and can keep up with him.

Unfortunately, this is one type that you really can't fake, it's not easy to play smart, that'll only make you appear dumb and backfire miserably. It is important to gain an affinity for literature, not your average novels or urban stories, I'm talking self-help books, some books on psychology and philosophy; even a few business books wouldn't hurt. This way you can expound on your opinions on different things that your target may be into.

The Intellectual has the power of his words at his disposal. Most people don't think before they open their mouths. A lot of people say the first thing that comes to their minds. Always remember that the person who interest us most is our own selves, keep this in mind when talking to your targets, women love to talk about themselves.

There is no seduction unless you get out of your own skin and into your target's. Intellectuals do this well because they are analytical, observant, and pay close attention to the details of their targets, gaining a feel of their psyche. Don't get too wrapped up in your own opinions and views, but use your intellectual stamina to confuse, delight, and stimulate your target. The difference between regular conversation and intellectual conversation is like the difference between noise and music. Most guys pull up and talk a bunch of noise. Its guaranteed for a CO to be bombarded with this on a daily basis. They normally tune this type of chatter out, but music is powerfully seductive and is widely used to sway the minds of the masses.

Music is intended for pleasure. A song can stay in your head for days. Its mesmerizing, even hypnotizing the way it alters our moods and arouses our emotions. Use your intellect to make music, not noise. Concoct phrases tailored to your victim that pleases them, things that relate to their lives, like little jewels they can use. Lightly stroke their egos in creative ways, or if you sense they have many issues in their lives (like most COs) then you can take their minds away from their problems with something witty and intellectually stimulating. You could paint a picture for them (include yourself in the vision) that makes the future seem hopeful. You must design dialog that is moving, detailed for them.

I will use one of my personal endeavors as an example of the Intellectual. In '12 I was at a smaller prison, they call them "county camps" here in Georgia. I was about three years into my bid at the time. The prison didn't have many female officers, only two or three, but all of the counselors were women.

A few months after I had arrived, a new counselor had started working there, her name was Mrs. Handler. Now, while all the other counselors were old and out of shape, Mrs. Handler was young and had it going on. She was a white girl in her early thirties, thick with a black girl ass, and was pretty as hell too. Needless to say, everyone was on her. Every time she would walk through the halls she was confronted by an inmate trying to get his mack on. I never paid her any attention. I noticed her, but never stared or showed any interest.

A few months of her being at the prison, I had my first interaction with her. I was coming in from an outside detail, walking down the narrow hallway alone. She came out of a door that was ahead of me and headed to her office door that was a bit further down. So now she's walking ahead of me but is aware that I'm a few steps behind. Her jeans were extremely tight, and she had on open toed high heels that clicked when she walked. She put extra sway in her hips, and her ass jiggled every step. Yeah, I was staring now.

When she reached her door, she turned to unlock it. As she inserted her key, she looked at me and spoke, "Hey, Ali. There was something that I needed to talk to you about. Can you think of what it was?" She asked me, her face in contemplation like she was trying to figure out what it was. Now, not only was I not even on this womans caseload, I had another counselor, but I didn't even know that she knew my name!

"Um, no. I can't think of what you would need to speak to me about." I replied, my voice low and smooth, no real expression on my face. She smiled. "Well, come in my office, we'll figure it out." I followed her as she led me in. I took a seat next to her desk. She sat her purse down and took a seat. Now in my mind, I already know that this chick is choosing, and is attracted to me. She made that quite obvious. There was no reason for her to speak to me, she wasn't my counselor. By her coming on to me, all I had to do was not screw this up, or say anything crazy, I already had her. She sat down then said, "Well, I can't think of why I needed to speak to you, but I got you in my office, that's not a bad thing right?" Her body language saying all the things her mouth couldn't.

"That's definitely a plus. What man wouldn't want to be alone in a room with you?" I said, playing along with her flirtatious game.

She studied her computer screen for a bit after asking me for my information, viewing my profile. She asked a few mundane questions about my crime, and why I was there. Then she ventured into my family and my past until we had gotten into other topics that clearly showed her interest in me.

I asked her a few questions of my own and got a chance to exhibit my intellectual side when we conversed about her college days. She was surprised by some of the books I'd read and how well I expounded on them, she could see that I wasn't an ordinary convict. We chatted that day for about forty-five minutes before I headed back to my dorm.

To my surprise, the next week she called me up to her office again. Now let me remind you, I wasn't on her caseload. I walked into her office and the first thing I noticed was, she was dressed like she had plans on spending a night out on the town. Her toes were out and her hair was done in a way that I'd never seen her wear before. That day we got into some deeper subjects. She asked me about Islam and told me how she had studied it in school. We discussed her college majors philosophy and psychology as well.

After that encounter she began to invite me up to her office at least twice a week. I could tell that she was thirsting for some intellectual stimulation in her life, something her husband couldn't provide. Sometimes women just want some conversation. Soon she was telling me about her marital issues, how she didn't feel desired any more, how her husband seemed to pay less and less attention to her. I knew where our little liaisons were headed, but I never jumped the gun, I let her set the pace.

Little contact on my hand evolved into strokes of my arm, which led to touches on my shoulder, until finally I could tell that she eagerly wanted me to kiss her, which I did. Her office was deserted, and we were always alone, we could easily have sex and get away with it, which eventually we did. I kept our sessions secret, telling no one, a rule that's often broken.

Eventually I began to lay seeds and insinuate how both of our financial situations could improve if she was willing to trust me and take some risk. It didn't take long for me to cultivate the right type of thoughts in her head, and sure enough she had come out and made the offer to me as if she had come up with the idea herself, the whole point in insinuating ideas. We made nearly fifty thousand dollars with phones, cigarettes and weed, and would've made more but I got transferred to another facility.

THE BACKFIRE

Although women tend to love an Intellectual Guy, you have to know who you're dealing with in prison. Most of the officers and other staff members are some country small town folk who probably barely made it out of high school, so you run the risk of talking over their heads. Therefore, make sure you gauge the person's intellectual level and dumb down your conversation if need be. Often times you will make the target feel inferior, or make them feel small, this will make them avoid you, so don't overdo it. Never make yourself too good to talk about some crazy topics that aren't anywhere near your interest, you'll have to endure this type of dialog sometimes, so just be patient with them, and don't spring on any subjects or concepts that may be difficult for your target to grasp.

THE PRETTY BOY

This type can be highly effective in prison if played correctly, but most individuals who fall into this type are unaware of how to use it. Most women in prison are already on alert to the game that inmates will try to run on them to manipulate them. So, their guards are up extra strong when an attractive male presents themselves to them, for this reason Pretty Boys have to maneuver more subtlety than any other type.

Pretty Boys have a self-made persona that excites women because ultimately, they can't be categorized. Sure, they can say this is a Pretty Boy, and he's probably a mack full of game, but they will become full of ambivalence because on one hand they know they should avoid him, but on the other they desperately want to be with him. So they can't place them in any category which leaves the target confused, right where you want her.

Pretty Boys have a freedom, a confident swagger that is often ambiguous and fluid. They are masculine and feminine at the same time, and also mysterious and elusive. Their physical image is often larger than life, and attracts attention, but seems effortless. They often go against the grain, paving their own lane.

Pretty Boys have a radical difference from everyone else, often thought of as homosexual by other inmates which is far from the truth, and often arousing jealousy from them. As most inmates are stuck within the confines of the roles they're forced to play, as gang members or tough guys, a lot of power is granted to the one who can be fluid and display their difference.

Most Pretty Boys are leaders, but not of official groups or specific gangs, but secretly people envy them, and want to follow and imitate them, even look up to them. Pretty Boys are rare in prison, most men would never dare present themselves in such a manor while in dangerous environments, hence the reason why they play tough and hard. Most people are insecure, which causes them to admire anyone who so freely expresses themselves in such a bold way. These types are uninterested in anything others have going on, and totally absorbed in themselves. This aloofness is one reason why women love them.

Pretty Boys are often associated by looks, and going the extra mile to look good, with hair grease and pressed clothes and the likes. One has to exhibit the proper attitude to go along with the outer appearance to fully embrace this type. One trait can't be effective without the other. His demeanor, his careless expressions and other characteristics has to go along with the look. But the clothing and style cannot be downplayed either. One must not try hard to stand out, or have a different style, Pretty Boys must be subtle and let the attention come to them, never going out of their way to get it. Trying too hard, or being flagrantly different will have a reverse effect, this shows lack of taste and women will not respect him.

An associate of mine named Mazi is a good example of a Pretty Boy. He was a civilian, or in other words he wasn't affiliated with any organization or gang. He was from Philadelphia, so his swagger was unusual just from that aspect. He was average height and really skinny, a light skinned guy with short dark curly hair that he usually wore in a temp fade. His voice was high pitched like a lot of dudes from up north, and his northern accent was very thick, and distinguished.

His uniforms were always extra white and crisp with sharp creases, and there were subtle details that stood out about the way he wore items. For instance, the tops of his shirt where the buttons stopped were always popped up and never laid down flat like everyone elses, and his shoe strings would be laced differently almost every day. He sported a lot of items that weren't prison issued, *'free world'* outfits like designer pajama sets and gym shorts, he had a nice gold chain with the *Five Percenter* emblem (he was a Five Percenter), a couple rings, a couple pair of nice *Cartier* glasses, and other beads that he wore on his wrist. He also had a couple pair of Jordan's which were rare, especially since they both were crisp and new.

He had told me of several officers he'd dealt with, but we were in the same dorm when I witnessed him work his magic with one. Her name was Ms.Norris. She, like most officers was a country chick from the middle of nowhere, a small town that didn't have much to offer. But she was a diamond in the rough, a real beauty. She was short, about 5'3, light skinned, and had a nice body. He had noticed her watching him a few times, but he had never spoken to her. She wasn't too friendly, she didn't converse much with inmates, but she was on a lot of people's radar.

It didn't take too long for Mazi to figure her out and how he'd approach her. He knew her guard would be up even more against guys like him, so he used a tactic I call "disqualification", this means that he came with something so off the wall that he made it certain that he wasn't trying to impress her, this has a major effect on lowering an officer's guard. He approached her for the first time, and said, "Hey, officer, come unlock my cell for me, I gotta take a shit!" Now as crazy as this sounds, it's a perfect way to disqualify yourself as a potential suitor. She gave him a look and wanted to laugh but kept her composure. That was their first contact.

A few days after that, a few guys were surrounding her, talking about whatever foolishness most inmates discuss. He pulled up to the group, boldly interrupted the conversation and said, "Hey man, fuck that shit y'all talking bout. You ever been in a wet T-shirt contest?" he asked Norris. She gave him a look, but shook her head no. He continued, "You ever kiss another woman?" She laughed at his remark and said no with a playful attitude. Then he said, "What color panties you got on? That's the kind of stuff I wanna talk to you about."

She smiled as he casually strolled off without another word. The other guys began to laugh at his comments and agree that those were the type of subjects they wanted to discuss as well. This type of approach is highly effective when dealing with most women, because its unexpected, and says a lot about the person who has the audacity to be that bold.

Mazi fell to the background after that encounter, waiting on her to make the next move, which she did a few days later. He was standing outside the dorm's door by himself as she walked up to him from behind. She touched his hand knowing physical contact between officers and inmates is a major violation. He faced her with a questioning expression on his face. "I wonder if you're the type of guy I think you are?" she said, peering into his eyes.

"I can see only one way for you to find out." he said. She walked back to her desk. The next day, he asked for her number, which she gave to him, and they talked frequently every day from that point on. He no longer said anything to her while she was at work, and he made it clear to her that they needed to keep it that way, cause people would surely talk and get jealous if they saw him conversing with her too often.

Norris was already money hungry, like most young people who aren't getting the pay grade that they want. So, Mazi was easily able to convince her that he had what it took to get them both paid. He painted a nice picture of what her life could be like if she took a chance on him, and they began working together. They had a run that lasted all summer, I know they had to have made about $80,000. She got caught on something that didn't have anything to do with them. They were good, no one suspected them of anything. One day the police were at the prison with K-9's, but they were after another chick.

Norris just happened to have a pack on her and the dogs sniffed it out. She was fired and arrested, but she never told on Mazi. They did the right thing and kept their activities secret, sometimes shit just happens.

THE BACKFIRE

As I mentioned before, Pretty Boy is a tricky angle to play. COs are already on high alert for guys to try and deceive them, and Pretty Boys are the main ones they try to avoid. So you have to make your approach extremely subtle. Learn from the techniques that Mazi used, those are good ways to get under an officer's skin without her knowing it. The trick is to say things that ensures them that you're definitely not trying to hit on them. Crack jokes on them, mention how bad their breath smells (even if it doesn't), say off the wall things, like tell them you have to take a shit real bad. Stuff like that lets them know that you can't be trying to impress them saying shit like that, and this will lower their guard towards you.

THE SNITCH

It's very rare that you will catch something by being this type. No one, even police, likes or respects a snitch. For one, officers who are willing to take risk will never trust you, you might tell on them! But, you do have avenues to use to your advantage.

Some officers are just not so smart, so they may feel that since you're a snitch, then you're on their team, and can actually gain their trust by being honest. Also, by you *"brown nosing"* the administration you'll get good details with the ability to work intimately close around staff and have a chance at getting in their heads and personal life, both key factors when getting an officer on your team. You can work this angle, but it can be highly dangerous if other inmates label you a nitch.

Another angle within this type is the "Institutionalized Guy", he usually gets labeled as a snitch by other inmates as well, so I included him in this category. This is your ideal model inmate. His clothes are always on point, shirt tucked in, pants up on his waist, room always in order and tidy, floors shined and waxed, etc. The administration knows him very well, and he carries a small level of respect from them, but not really.

He's *"jointed out"* as we say, by the book all the way through and through. Usually he's in everyone's business and very nosey, he'll be the one who has the news on everything happening around the prison. He's rarely a gang member, though sometimes he is, and he's normally been locked up for at least fifteen years, and probably not going home anytime soon. He's able to catch an officer simply because he understands prison and how it works. He is usually in a position of trust and can get details where he has a close relationship with officers, which is another reason why others will consider him a snitch.

He comes off as unthreatening because he's been down for so long and is more than likely older. But these types are very wise in the chain gang playing field, they've seen a lot in their experience. One problem with this type is that they may have an officer on the team but be afraid to use them because of their fear of getting in trouble. So, if you're this type, and you like to stay within the rules, you have to learn when it's wise to bend the rules a bit, especially when large sums of money are in question. If you decide to play this role, avoid the dangers of getting too far into character.

One of these types whom I've encountered was a guy named Jesse. Jesse was actually a high-ranking gang member, very rare to find one of these. Although I can't say for sure if he was a snitch, I can say that he was institutionalized.

In 2013, I had a detail working in the kitchen where I met Jesse. He was actually pretty cool, and we got along well. I noticed off the top that he took his job too seriously. These types often go the extra mile, being locked up so long with nothing better to do, it is easy to become engulfed in prison details. At this time, he had been down about twenty years and was going to get paroled out soon. He was a *"do boy"* for the director over the kitchen. She was an older woman named Ms.

Stanton. He would spend most of his time in her office going over inventory and other paper work. showing her how to save money as if he was a real employee.

I would often hear other inmates talking bad about him behind his back, saying that he was *"police"* and always with the director. I had even witnessed him do some police type shit, if he ever saw anyone stealing out of the kitchen, something inmates would do and sale the items back in the dorm, he would tell on them and get them caught. I once asked him why he did stuff like that. That's when he told me about his plan, he was willing to risk looking like a snitch in order to gain the trust of the director. He said that she was playing right into his hands, and soon she'd be bringing him phones. He told me that he played this angle at every prison he's been to. I asked if he was worried about what other inmates would do to him? He said he wasn't because he was a vet, he could fight really well, and he was a leader of a gang so no one would mess with him.

Sure enough, just as he'd planned, it didn't take long for him to accomplish his goals. He would give me large amounts of cigarettes and weed to sell, to help me get some money, which I made a lot of. Shortly after that, he was getting phones and we both made thousands of dollars.

I didn't really like the angle that Jesse played, but I had to respect it. He was getting phones in and selling them to me for low prices where I could make profits, so I wasn't mad at him. He confided in me and told me all of his business, like a lot of people tend to do with me, so I learned a lot of valuable lessons from him. He had a long run and had made over $40,000 before he had gotten snitched on by a real rat.

THE BACKFIRE

I mentioned most of the backfires and negatives to this type earlier, and there are plenty that you must avoid. This is by far the most dangerous type to try to play. In some prisons, you can even get killed if you're labeled a snitch, and the money you could make is not worth that. So, if you are this type, or want to take on this role, be extremely careful and know what type of environment you're playing in. Some prisons aren't that serious and tense, and you'll only be avoided and outcasted by other inmates instead of being beaten to death. So be aware of the dangers and move accordingly.

THE MONEY MAN

This is the most self-explanatory types, so I won't go too far in-depth with it. It's a well-known truth that everyone, especially women, are highly motivated and attracted by money, and seem to cling to those who have it. Therefore, The Money Man is very valuable and has an edge over other types. The problem then, is convincing your target that you have a substantial amount of money and doing it in a way that will get her to make money with you. There are so many guys who claim to have a *"check"*, and the officers have seen and heard it all, but there are various ways to show and prove.

The Money Man typically has a distinct demeanor about himself, the way he carries himself is often easy to tell that he has money, or at least used to. But this swag isn't always detected by the officers who work in prisons, so some tactful maneuvering on your part will be necessary. Having expensive accessories such as watches, or necklaces, may not be enough to convince your targets, but it helps.

You will distinguish yourself by your conversation as well, your confidence that exhibits a character who is accustomed to dealing with money and all that it brings. The Money Man is usually responsible and a natural leader, and he is rarely boastful and loud because he usually has nothing to prove. He will often take on traits of the Stand-Up Guy, who normally has money as well.

I've run into several Money Men throughout my bid, usually they had money on the streets, but sometimes their wealth was secured while in prison. One such individual was named Tech. He was a former pimp from the Lakewood area of Atlanta. He had caught two bodies when three armed men tried to rob him outside a strip club in Atlanta. He managed to shoot all three men and killed two of them. Luckily, he didn't get a murder charge and only ended up with manslaughter, which is a much lesser charge, since his case was self-defense.

I met him in 2014. He came into my dorm and stayed to himself for the first few weeks. He'd remain in his room all day reading novels. I had noticed his swag and figured that he was a Money Man by the way he carried himself. He also had several pairs of Tom Ford Sunshades, a long silver chain that hung to his waist, and a flashy watch that was worth a few thousand dollars. He was also really clean, all his clothes were pressed and kept up, even his pajama sets.

I met him because I had some cigarettes at the time, and he came to my room to shop with me, he bought a few singles, and we smoked one together before he left. Real recognized real and we became friends after that first encounter. He was also a Five Percenter and, me being an intellectual, we often had deep conversations.

I'd notice all the women watching him as we'd walk laps around the dorm. He had a magnetic disposition, real charismatic. But he'd never pay them any attention. Shortly after he'd arrived, he put up some money with me and another guy and we got a *'pack'* in together through an outside detail which included phones, and tobacce that we all split evenly.

Now that he had a phone, he set his sights on two officers who he'd thought would be open to working with him. One was a female, the other a male, but it was strictly business with the latter. He played a nice tactic with the female. He had several thousand dollars on his books (inmate account), nearly ten thousand. Whenever we purchased commissary, we'd receive a receipt showing the transaction details and remaining balances. His showed that he had thousands. So, he craftily approached the female with his receipt and complained about the commissary people claiming that he had no money, with the illusion that he wanted her help in the matter. He showed her his last receipt and she noticed his large balance. This was a way to indirectly show her a taste of what he was working with.

It didn't take him long to convince both of them of his networth, and how he could make them money. On separate occasions, he had $2,000 wired to both of them, kind of a down payment and a way to show he wasn't playing games.

With that, they both began to bring in contraband for him, the guy brought him weed and meth, and the girl brought phones. That continued to go well for months, but that wasn't all that he was involved in. He was still making moves with me and my guys on outside details, and he was getting packs in through the mail, and the warehouse. He had the whole compound on lock for a year, money was coming in from several streams, then he got transferred abruptly. Shortly after he left, he had the female officer dropping the phones off to me, and we continued a business relationship.

THE BACKFIRE

Being a Money Man really doesn't have any potential backfires. It may not always be easy to convince officers that you're for real, and really do have money, but that can be mounted in several ways. You also have to prepare for other guys to hate on you all the time, and it is inevitable that someone will snitch you out. So, you have to move accordingly and try not to make enemies. Other than that, The Money Man is a good type.

THE HOMO

Me personally, I am not homophobic, but my intel on this type is very limited. I included it because it is a reality in prison and they do catch a lot of women (and men) in prison. This is not my favorite type, but I said when I embarked on this project, that I would include all the elements of chain gang seduction that I knew of—the good, the bad, and the ugly.

So, homosexuals are not only a part of the equation but, actually, you'll find that most officers are willing to work with them, thus bringing them a lot of power behind the walls. I've seen institutions where the homosexuals ran the prison and were getting all the money.

As I've mentioned in earlier chapters, females, like most humans, love familiarity, and they are attracted to what makes them comfortable and feel secure, and homosexuals do just that, in a highly effective manner. Homosexuals tend to consider themselves women when they are of the feminine kind, therefore they can relate to women in a way that most men can't. This opens the door for them to maneuver within the minds of their targets.

Homosexuals have a positive way of getting their targets to drop their guards, one of the most difficult aspects of seduction. Also, homosexuals rarely care what others think of them. They've been criticized their whole lives, so they've developed a high level of tolerance against naysayers, which has made them learn to accept themselves for who they are. This high level of freedom is powerfully seductive and they use it effectively.

Often times a woman will befriend a homosexual quicker than anyone else because they'll feel like a homosexual does not have an ulterior motive. They come off as genuine and appear not to be hiding anything. So they're comfortable with giving them casual conversations that lead to them educating their targets on the ends and outs of prison, then finally how much money can be made. By this time, the woman has trusted them, so it was easy for him to manipulate her.

I have only dealt with one homosexual, and that was on a business level. His name was Carlos, and though I did'nt share many detailed conversations with him, I was still able to pick up a few jewels by watching him. I watched as he jumped on every new officer that started working. They'd befriend him, he'd fill them in on prison life, and gossip a bit to entertain them. Then before you knew it, they were working together.

THE BACKFIRE

There really aren't many backfires to this type, for some reason women just love homosexuals, and they actually get more officers than any other type. All I can say is, there may be some women who are just repulsed by that lifestyle, but that doesn't stop much because there are more women that don't mind it at all.

THE LADIES' MAN

The Ladies' Man is a true seducer. This is his essence. He's a major manipulator, covering his deceptions with pleasure and comfort. His approach is quite simple. He merely takes attention away from himself and focuses it on his target. He naturally understands the nature of women and their spirits, he feels their pain, and he adjusts to their moods. When he's in the presence of women, he makes them feel better about themselves, he uplifts them, making it hard not to love him, even when they know he's a Ladies man.

A Ladies Man doesn't argue or fight, they don't complain, and this is seductive in itself. They have a way of drawing women in and making them dependent on them, strengthening his power over them. They also aim at women's ultimate weaknesses, vanity and self-esteem.

A Ladies' Man will focus on fulfilling the aspects of seduction that are alluring and addictive, the attention, the boost of reassurance, the illusion of understanding. But underneath it all, is the lurking presence of sexual tension.The Ladies' Man's power is in his ability to capture a women's attention while lowering their sense of reason at the same time. He strikes at the things women have the least control over, their emotions, their egos, and self-esteem.

One of the keys to seduction is learning to cater conversations to your target because women love talking about themselves and this is what the Ladies' Man does best. But he must never operate too obviously, for this kills any seduction, subtlety is highly important in any seduction. Therefore, a light touch is best, and not bombarding your target with compliments every time you see her.

I've met several Ladies' Man types during my bid, but the one who was expert at what he did was a guy named Philly. I met Philly early in my sentence and he taught me a lot. I noticed how comfortable he was in his own skin, and how he interacted with women, flowery speech just flowed from his tongue as if he had planned his encounters with them, though he never did. One of the things he told me was to get the target used to talking to you, get her comfortable with you, and never come on too strong too early. He would hit his targets with a little taste of his charm, then push on and go about his business. The words he left them with made them stand up a bit straighter after he'd left, as if he'd dropped a cup of confidence on them. He made them feel good about themselves, which in turn, made them want to be around him more.

Another thing I noticed about Philly was that unlike most seductive types, who focus on one target at a time, Philly would interact with all the women he could, making every encounter a potential seduction. Now normally this kind of activity would backfire, making the women feel like you just hit on everyone and they're not really special, but with him it actually worked in his favor. In the minds of the officers, it was looked at as an insult if he never flirted with you. They took it as if something was wrong with them. By doing this, he made virtually every female officer vie for his attention. They ate up every word.

Once, Philly had gotten a detail working in laundry. There was a mediocre looking woman who ran laundry, her name was Ms. Wright. She was average at best, a basic looking black woman, with no life to speak of. But Philly brought her to life. He'd shower her with compliments, noticing the small touches that no one else ever really commented on— her hands, her neckline, the elegant way that she formed sentences. These statements from him made her glow, because they appeared to be genuine. He couldn't comment on her looks, for she had none, that would've made her suspicious. So instead, he opted to notice other qualities she possessed.

It didn't take long for Ms. Wright to become more and more enraptured by his company. She thirsted for his conversation and looked forward to it every day she came to work, which lead to her work hours not being enough, and as you can imagine, she brought him a phone so they could talk while she was off.

THE BACKFIRE

Often times you'll run into officers that are quite immune to the Ladies' Man and know their tricks. Sometimes you'll even have those women who are confident enough to not need any validation. These types will see through your plots and view you as deceptive and sneaky. The way to solve this is to work on as many people as possible. Take the example of Philly and make it your reputation to hit on officers, make them want to be your victims.

THE REPELLER

Just as we all possess character traits that attract others, we all possess certain traits that repel people. Having knowledge of these traits within ourselves and working to remove them is just as important as cultivating the attractive qualities within us. Unfortunately for most of us, we exhibit more anti-seductive traits naturally than we do the seductive ones. This in turn makes people, especially women, try to stay away from us. In the following paragraphs I go over a few of the repelling traits, you must be honest with yourself and do some self-reflecting, weed out the traits that you notice, and weed out the people in your life who act in these ways.

The Repeller comes in various types, but they're very easy to spot and quite easy for you to recognize within yourself. While they differ in the manifestations, they all share the same result, they make people want to stay away from us and dread being around us. Another common trait, which serves as the source to the problem, is insecurity. Don't get me wrong, we are all usually insecure to some degree, but some of us suppress our insecurities better than others, and those who are full-fledged repellers exude these traits to the full extent making it virtually impossible for them to ever catch or seduce an officer.

It is of utmost importance to stay away from these types of people, contact with them can dampen your soul and cause you to embrace some of their traits, remember, character is contagious. There are signs to look for to indicate that you're befriending a repeller—stinginess, always talking about others behind their backs, being heavily judgmental, they love to argue passionately and emotionally about the most frivolous topics. Sometimes they pledge their loyalty and love to you when you've only just met them and it's clear that their words cannot be sincere. These are only some of the traits to identify the Repeller by. Pay close attention to those whom you allow into your intimacy.

Recognizing the many qualities of The Repeller in ourselves and removing them from our personalities will raise our seductive potency to a much higher level providing more chance for us to catch. We all have these traits, so do not be arrogant and believe that you are above suffering from them. Here are some of the traits that I've ran into from my experiences:

The Bogard: This type has no finesse, no patience. They try to muscle in or force themselves into beneficial situations no matter the cost. The art of catching these officers takes tact and patience, one that the bogard never practices. They may have their way at times, but they suffer in the end. They have an over inflated ego and feel that they are superior to everyone and that we own them, but deep inside they really feel inferior and dread the thought of anyone finding out their true identity.

The Clinger: These are among the worst in my personal opinion. They become so thirsty for attention that they're always in the target's face, never giving her time to breathe. They can't take hints that its past time for them to allow for some space, so they continue with their ploy until eventually they run the target off and ruin any chance that they may have had of catching her.

The Rigid: These are usually over-religious types, among others. They are so engulfed in their own ideas and beliefs that they have become closed-minded and have indirectly closed themselves off from the world and its benefits. Although it is good to be firm in your beliefs and what you stand on, you never want to take this good quality too far. Too much of anything will kill you. What's worst is when they try to force you to bend to their will and convert to their beliefs, this is when they've become very overwhelming. They want to change everyone. Feeling that their way of life is correct, and everyone else's ideals are wrong, so it's their duty to save the world all that they come in contact with. Their intentions may be good, wanting to make you a better person, but their methods are far from correct. What lies beneath this type though, is a deep-seated unhappiness covered by their need to dominate those around them. Although this type is self-exposed and easy to spot, you will also notice their stiff physical stature, as if a stick ran up their spines.

The Crab: The only indicator of the crab is its outer manifestation. Stinginess has more to do with not giving money, but it stems deeper than that. What lies beneath the surface is an inability to let go, to take risk, maybe they've lost a lot in their childhood, but something has them afraid to open up and give themselves to the world so they horde whatever they get their hands on. Some will try to prove that they're not stingy, so they may give a crumb here and there, but you can bet that they'll do it in the open where others will know of their deeds. This type is overprotective of themselves, and to catch you have to open up and be willing to give freely of yourself.

I personally despise these, they may be the worst type. This type feels like they're always right, and what they have to say is all that matters. They dominate any conversations they engage in, rarely allowing anyone to get a word in. They are extremely rude, cutting people off when someone else makes a statement. If you try to talk over them, they only get louder until you are battling over who can talk the loudest and they will always win. They love to hear themselves talk, often telling long drawn out stories including every minute detail, not realizing the boredom that they induce on those around them. When they are faced with a target, they only speak of themselves, being the least interested in what she has to say or what's on her mind. They have a deep-seated selfishness, this is usually the root and source. When these types come around, I always have an escape route on hand, as they are quite unpleasant.

The Oversensitive: These are those who take things far too seriously. They overreact when anyone jokes with them or something to that nature. They feel like everyone is taking shots at them, or indirect or ambiguous statements were meant for them. They often complain about nothing and whine all the time. They feel like everyone is against them, and they're victims. They love to bask in their own misery. It is best to go with the flow and never take things personally. Let insults roll off your shoulders, you're too cool to be affected by someone's punchlines, but these types are unable to do that, they take everything personally.

The Gossiper: This type is quite like the Motormouth, but they have their differences. This type is always heard in public, they're obnoxious to a fault, and can't keep their mouths shut. They disclose everyone's business, never exposing their own, and always talk behind other people's backs, even those whom they declare to be friends. You can't trust them to any extent, and if they find out about some secret of yours, you'd better believe that everyone else soon will. They are always people's go-to person for information, which is often inaccurate. If they converse with officers, more than likely they are bad mouthing someone else, which little do they know, they're only making themselves look bad along with whomever they're discussing.

These types are a few who I've run across and analyzed. It is detrimental to your goals if you continue to exude these traits. Study them, as well as any other characteristics that I haven't covered, and remove them from your persona. It may not work over night, but continuous effort and catching yourself when you notice that you are acting in an undesired way will have a major effect in eventual betterment of your character. Arm yourself with the seductive traits and destroy any repelling traits.

PART TWO
THE TARGETS

In order to have a better success rate at seduction, it is important to choose the right target. Choosing the proper target consist of knowing or having a general idea of what your target wants. It wouldn't be wise to try to catch fish with chocolate on a hook. Its more fitting to use worms or other insects that attract fish. In the same light, it is far more effective to present yourself in a manner that will be appealing to your target.

I have provided the second phase of the book with brief descriptions of select types of targets typically found in prisons. As I mentioned in the introduction, this is only from my experience and there are possibly many other types that I failed to mention. While studying this section, pay attention to the needs or wants of each type. This is the most important point of your approach. Not all seductive types can catch any target. Some targets are more susceptible to particular seductive types. For instance, "The Girlfriend" may be more open to getting involved with "The Flashy Guy" because she sees the attention that he gets from other women, and she wants him for herself or the "Dime Piece" may be more open to the "Pretty Boy" because his looks may be more acceptable to her.

You may notice that most targets will fall into more than one category, as most people often do. In these instances, look for the traits in them that stick out the most. As you get better acquainted with the target you'll find the dominant character traits that they exude, then act accordingly.

In most of the types, I have provided little details to look for in order to identify them. Also, I provided different ways to approach them in order to better plan your actions. Seduction is war in a sense, so it's best to plan, then execute your plan with the strategies that you've tailored for your target. Get to know these types, it is essential to your success.

THE HELPER

Most women have an innate desire to help people—sort of a nurturing side to them. When they see someone, anyone in need, they generally want to aid them, or do what they can for them. I call these Helpers, and there's plenty of them in prisons.

Usually this type will be older women, but not always. Sometimes they come in any age. Even though she may sincerely want to help when she sees you in need, she's not gonna act on that impulse. So, you still have to put in work to get to know her, let her know you need her help, and what she can do for you. The poor and needy are the perfect types for these, because you don't want to appear like you've got it all together, then you don't need help. With these, its best to appear needy and they'll want to rush to the rescue.

THE DIME PIECE

This type can be tricky in prison. On the streets it's obvious who's a dime and who isn't, but in prison, there's rarely any real dimes working. Dimes are those who are just a touch prettier than the rest, therefore they get a lot of attention and compliments from inmates who boost their heads up. Thus they develop a "Dime Piece" mindset, even though in reality they're not that pretty. Don't let their high headed attitude fool you, these types are usually very insecure. It's easy to spot them because a lot of guys will like them and talk about them often, but understand the best approach with these is to never compliment them when you first start dealing with them. They have inmates flirting with them and compliment them all day, so the worst thing you can do is hit them with the same ol' material they hear so often.

In my experience, you have two choices: you can lightly diss them, but in a playful way, not so harsh to where you offend them. Just make them laugh a little and take some shots back at you, or you can come with something that's extra original, something they've never heard before.

THE BITTER LEADER

Usually these types are a part of the administration and it takes a mature individual to catch their attention, though not all the time. There are exceptions to every rule. Stand-Up Guys and older guys are usually the ones to attract them. These are a bit difficult to catch, but the trick is to treat them differently. Everyone around them tends to want something from them, which makes them skeptical and questioning the motives of everyone. They're usually a little tough and hard around the edges, but deep down you'll find a softer reality. These types yearn to be seduced, especially if they're older, which they tend to be. They need someone to overwhelm them, make them feel different about themselves, something no one around them does.

Unfortunately, most inmates are too afraid to make any attempts towards them. The trick, then, is to treat them like you're their equal- or even superior! This is a feeling they rarely receive, it'll arouse a great interest in them. Be direct with your approach, but tactful at the same time so you don't end up in the hole. Tell them about themselves, be harsh, and firm, but follow it up with a softer touch on your next interaction.

This is probably the most difficult target as they are overly suspicious, and smarter than most. Also, their minds are filled with burdens and duties, leaving little room to be tricked. You'll have to be diligent and consistent, slowly filling their thoughts with you. You can bet that they're lonely, and when you do succeed, the benefits will be well worth the effort.

THE STRICT POLICE

Every prison is full of these. They are the ones who take their jobs way too seriously. On the surface it appears as if there's no getting to them, but the reality is quite the contrary. In fact, you'll discover that these tend to be the ones who work with inmates the most. Plus, they're among the best to work with since no one will suspect them of doing anything.

Your approach is similar to the way you'll approach the Bitter Leader. These types normally won't give much conversation to inmates, but there are ways to get them to open up. One way is to act like an "institutionalized" convict, and realize that often times, the officers who work in prisons are institutionalized themselves. You can start by talking about chain gang stuff and see how far that gets you.

Once you've gotten them used to talking to you, you can slowly divert the dialogs to other subjects, but never come on too strong, they're vets at this so they'll read game from a mile away. Once you get into their personal lives you can pretty much get them on your team. Once there, make sure they maintain their hard exterior of being a Strict Police. This attitude will keep everyone thrown off.

THE UNHAPPY

These are the types who used to dream and hold high ideals about how they imagined their life would be when they became adults.

Unfortunately, they didn't meet their childhood fantasies and fell extremely short from their marks. Most people fall into this category and a lot of them work in prisons. No one ever dreamed of becoming a CO when they were kids, this is usually where people go when they don't have many other options.

You can assume that the majority of the employees at your facility fall into this group, but it's better to make sure that they are in fact lacking in their lives and a strong desire for something more. You can feel them out by books they may read, stories about other people's ideal lives, or t.v. shows they watch— the ones that paint life as a perfect picture. They want the dreamy husband, and the carefree lifestyle of wealth and abundance.

These types are often married with a few kids and stuck in their unhappy situation. It is fairly easy for you to pry into their personal lives and provide a nice change of pace to their drab existence. Make off handed comments about your life before prison. Make up stories about how perfect everything was for you and lay it on thick. It's good to make up an alternative reason to why you're there, make it seem as if it wasn't your fault and you were trying to help a friend. Make yourself the victim and make the story sound pathetic.

Don't worry if they are married, their spouses are often the source of their resentment, whether that's true or not. Just be sure to fill their minds with passion and adventure. Lead them to believe that you can be the one to provide that lifestyle. Maybe even hit them with a few lines of poetry, romance them a bit. That is more than likely foreign to them, something their husbands never do. Get them to talk about what they really want from life, what career would they choose if they could be anything. Let them spill their guts, while they talk they'll be in another world, if only for the moment. But soon, they'll associate you with all the blissful feelings that they've been experiencing.

THE HUSTLER

Most people consider themselves Hustlers. However true that is, it's not your concern. It's your job to sniff out the so-called

Hustler and exploit their beliefs about who they think they are. In today's time, with the main topic of popular music, everyone is a boss, and a hustler, or at least they aspire to be. This is the mindset of a lot of prison employees.

The Hustler will more than likely be those who haven't been on the job for that long. They probably view this as a short-term gig and a temporary inconvenience. You can detect them by their seriousness, and no bullshit demeanor. Your talks with them should be more direct than with any other target. Once you've developed a rapport with them, you can come at them with a straight up business proposition. Inform them of the possibilities, the potential money to be made, and the easy ways to bring in what you need.

It's important that your demeanor matches theirs, you should carry yourself responsibly, like a grown man, a businessman, and leave the kiddy shit to another target. Sometimes you have to be patient with them, let them get a feel of the job, let them contemplate the risk. Don't be too pushy.

These types will definitely end up working with someone, your job is to make sure it's you.

THE TEMP

You'll find quite often that the young women that work in prisons are often in school or working another job that is more important to them. These are what I call "Temp", and they are one of the easiest targets to catch. Since they are working towards a more promising and fulfilling carcer, they tend to be more eager to take risk to earn money, because to them this job is only temporary.

Most of these types are more ambitious and money hungry which leads them to be more eager to work with you. Usually they're smarter than most officers, more focused and driven, which makes them better to work with because they can think for themselves without you needing to guide their every move.

It's not always easy to spot these by their physical characteristics. Like most targets, you'll have to indulge in some innocent conversation and probe into their personal lives. Sometimes you can gather information about them from other convicts or officers, though sometimes these sources can be inaccurate. Once you've gathered enough info, you can start your pursuit.

THE PLAYER

Being a corrections officer isn't the most glamorous job. Like a lot of jobs, it's full of daily routines that always lead to boredom. In turn, you have a lot of officers that just like to play and kick it to pass their time. Don't let these types fool you, they're usually quite friendly and will talk with pretty much anyone. This kind of social behavior will lead many to believe that she can easily get manipulated into working with a convict. The truth of the matter is, this is far from the truth. Players are among the most difficult to catch.

You'll notice different people in their face all the time, but she's not intending on doing business with any of them. She has only one thing on her mind and that's to pass time. To her, you're just there for her entertainment, and nothing more.

Though it is rare to catch this type, it's not impossible. My advice is to avoid them. It's not worth wasting valuable time trying to convince them to get some money, when there's likely to be many others in your realm that you can work on.

THE VET

Many officers have been working on the job for several years while at the same time working for themselves. These are the best ones to get on your team, yet one of the more difficult because they're smart, they haven't survived for years by being stupid. This leads them to be extremely picky about who they choose to work with.

The Vets are almost always gonna be older, more mature officers. Sometimes they have a little rank, maybe sergeants, lieutenants, or higher but not all the time. Sometimes they're still regular COs who've just been on the job for years but never wanted to move up in rank because they've been getting so much money on the side.

This type isn't gonna work with just anyone. It'll take Stand-Up Guys or Intellectuals to get them. They're about their business so they want those who are serious and seem to be about their business as well. This type isn't always easy to spot, but if you have an older officer who's been working for a while, chances are she's willing to do some business. Just feel her out and drop subtle hints and see if she bites.

THE ADVENTURER

Like the Player, Adventurers are bored with the drudgery of their lives. Unlike the Player, Adventurers are ready and willing to participate in something taboo just for the thrill of it. They like to live dangerously, on the edge, and care very little about making money or having a relationship or fling. Pay attention to your conversations with them and see how their faces light up whenever you mention something adventurous and wild. This is how you catch this type. Sometimes they'll complain about their lives and how it doesn't offer any excitement. Sympathize with them and draw out all of their pent-up dissatisfaction, making them want to live out their dreams through you.

THE GIRLFRIEND

These types are typically the easiest to manipulate. They're usually desperate, starving for attention, and they stick out and are easy to spot and easy to place them in this category. More than likely they are not attractive, are single and alone, and get no attention on the street or in prison.

One of the best things about this type is that they'll recognize that you're running game on them, trying to seduce them, especially if you're a Ladies' Man or a Pretty Boy-but they won't even care. They'll be so thrilled and loving the attention they're getting from you, that the thought of being desired and the feelings of excitement will keep them eating out of the palm of your hand, despite the fact that they know there's no way that you can genuinely be interested in them. With that being said, and as easy as they are to catch, you still don't want to lay it on too thick, especially not early on. At first, it may be good to give them a few seductive stares.

Nothing creepy, just some light eye contact to show them that you're into them. Then, depending on how they react to that, you can pull up with mundane conversation. Something light and casual, trying not to hit on them or compliment them on features that they clearly don't have. Like saying they look good when it's obvious they don't. Trust me, they know they don't and it would be good to try to act like you're a bit shy yourself, this will make them more comfortable.

After you've gotten them used to you pulling up and talking with brief convo, then you can point out little things about her that may be attractive. Maybe she has a nice ass or toned physique or maybe she has nice lips. But gauge her reactions to your come ons, this will show you how light or heavy you should be. Of course, if she laughs or smiles then you know you're on the right track.

Try to open up to her a bit. Tell her some good stories from your past, about your plans and ambitions. More importantly, get her to do most of the talking. Your goal is to get her to a point where she views you like her boyfriend. So it's your job to direct your interactions to that place. Once you've got her to that point, it's time to get her number.

Now this is where it can get tricky. Most people assume that if a chick is attracted to you, and wants to be your girl, that she's guaranteed to bring you stuff. That's a wide spread misconception. Even after you've gotten her in love with you, you still have a lot more finesse to lay down before she does that. I've seen plenty of guys get the girl, talk to her on the phone, maybe even kiss and hug them all the time, yet they never get her to bring the pack and that's a crying shame! The goal is the money! Relationships are cool too, if you're lonely, but that's not your primary objective, unless it is, then you're reading the wrong book.

Also, Girlfriends can easily be confused as Players. Players will lead you on like they want to get involved with you, but in the end, they just want you to entertain them with stimulating conversation while they do their eight hour shift. Players can be distingsished by people they talk to and kick it with. They'll talk to nearly anyone! A true Girlfriend will pretty much limit herself to the one she's chosen and hopefully that's you, for fear that talking with too many people will make you angry. So be aware of the difference.

MALE OFFICERS

You may be surprised to find out that male officers are usually easier to work with than women and in most cases they're easier to convince. They will fall into the same categories as I've listed already, such as the Unhappy, The Hustler, or The Adventurer. Approach in much the same way once you've identified who they are.

Male Officers can be easier to catch because their guards aren't up as high as women's. You can pull up and spark a conversation more easily and the dialog will flow with less effort on your part. Talk about things that men love to talk about, women, sports, cars, etc. Make it your business to stay in his face as often as you can. In this instance, you don't have to be delicate and not come on too strong as you do with women.

Feel your target out as thoroughly as you can, and learn what type of guy he is, then tailor your strategy accordingly. Most men think they know it all, so don't be afraid to let him lead, or at least create the illusion that he's leading. Allow him to use his intellect and give you information on things you may not have known. Don't let the egos clash between the two of you.

Sometimes you can just have a male CO on the team, but not exactly bringing anything. A lot of these guys want to feel cool and not be viewed as police. They're more open to prove themselves to you by telling you things that are about to happen, future shakedowns, who's snitching and things like that. You can also build a little network with them to help the female officer bring stuff in, they can be a little team.

Also, some of them may be gay so beware of that. They may want to be more than *"cool"* with you. But that's your business.

Personally, I wouldn't get involved with them since leading them on could end in disaster when they discover you're not really gay. I've known guys to play that angle and be successful. They'll play the role. but usually will just exchange suggestive words with them, but never really do anything physical with them. Words are bad enough if you ask me, but it's your call. It can be beneficial if played correctly.

PART THREE
THE STRATEGIES

After you've discovered what type of seducer you are, and you've evaluated the character of your target. Now it's time to tailor your approach. There are several ways to maneuver and get into officer's heads. I have included several in the following chapters. You may know of others to add to your arsenal, these are only the ones that I have witnessed work effectively during my experiences. Some tactics are only good for specific targets and some are universal. Study this section thoroughly and design the best approach for your plan.

THE SAVER

This strategy is very effective if you use it correctly and on the right target. Most young girls will fall for this trick, but it's not wise to attempt it with vets who are more than likely familiar with this approach. The Saver is when you make yourself appear to be on the side of the target and create the illusion that you're only looking out for their best interest. This tactic is typically played by Stand-Up Guys and gang leaders but can also be applied by other seductive types.

Although there are a few different ways to act as a Saver, the main one is this: get someone to play along with your scheme. If you're in a gang it's best to get someone from another gang to make it more believable. If you use someone within your gang, your target may suspect the setup.

The trick is to get your guy to purposefully bother the target. Get him to arouse an argument with her, the more heated the argument, the better. Its best to do it where not many people will see, so that no other inmates will get involved. Once the arguing has reached a certain point, you step in and stand up for the target. You defend her and appear to be extremely angry at the way your guy is talking to her. Make sure to yell at him and warn him not to speak to her that way. Make him argue with you, then the two of you go to a cell as if you're going to fight.

If your cell doors can close without bars where onlookers can see through, then you two can just bang the lockers or bang the walls, whatever it takes to make it seem like you're fighting. After a few moments, throw some water on your face like sweat, take your shirt off, and exit the room, making sure your target saw the whole thing.

Breathe somewhat heavily, but not too excessively, like you barely won, but just enough to make it believable. For extra effectiveness, approach the target if she's still around and let her know you handled that for her. Inform her that you've got her back whenever she needs you. After this, your target will be more inclined to trusting you.

THE BACKFIRE

Make sure before you try this that you choose a target that won't call in the incident, then you may find yourself in the hole. Some officers may get spooked if they think you're fighting and call in a code and have officers storming in. So be mindful of that. Also, if you're attempting this with an opposing gang member, you may want to run it by a member with some authority. If his fellow members aren't aware of what's going on, they'll think you two are serious and a conflict is sure to ensue. So beware of that. Now, letting others into the move also brings more people into your business and that's usually an issue in itself, so select the right people. Never tell them more than necessary.

THE JACK MOVE

I know what might come to mind when you first hear the heading of this strategy. You're wrong. I'm not referring to robbing, or jacking in the traditional usage of the term. When I say "The Jack Move", I'm actually referring to masturbating on female officers. Now, if you are in prison, chances are you are well aware of what I'm talking about and how this is a regular occurrence in prison. Men in prison, being heavily deprived of any sexual activity, often resort to masturbating while watching female officers. As perverted as this may sound, it is a common thing.

What makes this interesting is that some women in the system actually enjoy the activity. Most women are repulsed by it, and feel highly disrespected when this happens, and are quick to get you sent to the hole for pulling your piece out in their presence. But there is a large number who don't mind, and even some who like it.

I've even known guys who have pulled officers by jacking on them. It is rare, but it is a reality that has happened. One thing you must remember is that women are often insecure, no matter how confident they may seem. Also, most women love to feel desired by a man, even if it's in a psycho perverted manner. By a man being able to ejaculate simply by the sight of a woman, this can have a positive effect on the mindset of the woman. She may be flattered or even feel desired that a man, especially if you're a handsome guy, can achieve this level of arousal by her presence alone.

This is not hard to believe when you consider that most officers in a prison tend to have a certain level of mental health issues as well as the inmates. So don't be afraid to utilize this approach. This tends to work well with women who don't normally get much attention. The fact that you find them sexy enough to jack to them can be highly attractive to them and even turn them on in the process. It's a matter of knowing who you're dealing with.

Sometimes it's good to talk to the woman first and get a feel of who she is. You can even ask her first how she feels about you jacking on her. Though sometimes it's more effective to just go for it and take a chance, the audacity may be viewed as bold, a seductive trait in itself.

It's usually not likely that you'll pull an officer who let's everyone jack on her, there's nothing special or different in that case. Find one who no one jacks on and make something exclusive between the two of you.

THE BACKFIRE

This strategy is more repulsive than attractive, nine times out of ten. It's extremely risky and usually isn't the best idea, although I've seen it work for others. I have seen this approach backfire more than any other though. Most women feel very uncomfortable when you do this. Sometimes they may have been into you and would've given you some play, but now that you've whipped your dick out and showed her, she's totally turned off by you. She will view you like every other creep you're locked up with. So, if you do this, understand the risk, and if you have a target that you know is feeling you, I suggest you don't go this route unless you see how she feels about it first.

THE TRINITY

I call this strategy "The Trinity" because it typically involves three people: you, a co-conspirator, and the target. Not only is this a highly effective strategy, but it is one of the more respectable ones. In seduction, or picking up women in any setting, it's good to have a wingman of some sort. In prison, it works a bit differently. How it's mainly done is this: you discover, usually by subtle signs, that an officer is attracted to an inmate, whether it's you or someone you know. Before the one who she's digging approaches her, you send in the wingman.

It is his job to soften her up for you, cultivate the playing field so to speak, and get it ready for growth. As he's chatting her up about mundane topics, he subtly insinuates good characteristics about the guy who she's into. But this must be made as subtly as possible. Say for example, the conversation was men in prison and how most can't take care of their children while they're incarcerated. You may say, "Yeah, it's hard to handle your responsibilities in here. I only know a couple of guys who really handle business are able to send money to their kids. In fact, my homeboy 'so and so', that's my bro, he always sends money and maintains a bond with his kids". That's just an example of how you can work your friend in the conversation without coming straight out and talking good about him and not sound crazy or gay.

What'll be more shocking to her is that she's so used to hearing guys down talk other guys, it'll be a positive change of pace to hear someone talk about another in a positive light. Usually when guys talk about other inmates they're hating and gossiping about another man. He's only making himself look bad, along with the person he's backbiting. This happens way too often.

You want to mention the other guy's qualities one time, or two at the most but on two different occasions, not twice in the same conversation. That'll be too obvious and she'll more than likely see through it. If done right, you can indirectly paint a nice picture of the person whom she is already into and further his chances of catching her. Once you've properly laid the ground work, you can let him do his thing. Sometimes she'll even initiate some interactions with him herself. Then you know you made an impact.

THE BACKFIRE

If done properly, this is hard to mess up. At the most she'll think you're dick-riding, but that won't have a negative effect on the guy she likes, only on the wingman. If your insinuations aren't subtle enough, she may mistake you two as homosexuals and that would be a major setback. So, just be sure to tailor your approach and have in mind exactly what you're going to say. That will help in the end and that way you won't have much to worry about.

MANUAL SUGGESTION

This tactic is heavily important in any type of seduction and cannot be over stressed. You would think that a good approach would be to come straight out and tell your target what's on your mind and your intentions with them. That seems honest and noble, but that never works in real life. In real life, no one really wants to hear the truth or hear your true intentions. So, it's always best to shield your intentions through the secret world of insinuating or suggesting your ideas to others.

In prison, it's easy for your target to detect your mind games, so you can never make it too obvious. They're already suspicious of you anyway, so convicts have to work extra hard to lower our target's defenses against us. The good thing is that there is no defense against insinuations. This is a shadowy language that speaks to your target's subconscious leaving them unaware of exactly what you said, but your seeds will take root in their minds and sprout days later. If done effectively, you can actually make them think the idea was originally theirs.

This is the ultimate sub-language: statements with vague meanings, mundane talk filled with seductive glances, body language. All of this and more enters your target's subconscious mind and relates to them your true meaning. This will take some patience and tact, but all seduction in prison does. In the end, it will be well worth it.

The practice is quite simple, its merely dropping subtle hints to your target disguised in an innocent statement that is ambiguous and could be taken in different ways. The topic of the hint should aim at your target's known insecurity: a lack of adventure and excitement in their lives; some emotional issue; or my personal best, their lack of financial security. The comment will register in their minds. Often times the person who brought it up (you) will be forgotten as its source and can't figure out why their minds are preoccupied with how to get more money.

Your statements must allude to what you want the target to know without you coming straight out and saying it. If you tell them all about the thousands of dollars you ran through on the street, they probably will not believe you and it'll go in one ear and out the other, but if you tailor your speech, tell stories about places where only a person with money goes, mention hanging out with known individuals that get money, these statements will go a lot further.

It must not be in a boastful manner though—only kicking it and having conversation. Khadafi, a friend of mine, used to have fake commissary receipts printed out with a false balance of twenty thousand or so. Then he'd approach a CO with complaints about his commissary, knowing she can't do anything about it. He'd then show her his last receipt knowing she'd see the large balance. In this way, he showed her he had money without directly telling her.

Its best to make your statements vague, make them off-handed comments, and then quickly change the subject as if you didn't mean for that statement to slip out. Later on, your target will dwell on what you said, trying to find meaning to it. Make your statements stab at your target's secret desires, their little-known yearnings that you picked up from your talks with them. Paint the picture as if you can offer the release they need. The key is to make them come to you and make them offer their aid to you, as if they are the ones plotting now. In this way you change the dynamic, they are now seeking you out.

Also, it is equally important to utilize your gestures and body language as well. Sometimes it's not what's said with your words that your targets pick up on. The look in your eye speaks volumes when used correctly. Watch your demeanor around other inmates when your target is around. Maintain an air of power and leadership, assume this position and people will believe it even if it's not necessarily true. This topic is of the essence and must be mastered if you want success in your plans. You will never succeed if you always approach your targets with your plans of getting money with them off the rip. Be subtle, be sneaky, learn to bypass their suspicions and speak directly to their impressionable subconscious.

EFFECTIVE WORD PLAY

You've heard this saying a million times, "Conversation rules the Nation", and it's as true in seduction as it is anywhere else. The conversation I'm now referring to is more so directed to the power of words! Word play has a powerfully influential effect on all people, but more so on women.

Most people never really think before they speak and end up saying things they shouldn't have. It's natural to utter the first things that come to our minds, but this can be disastrous when trying to get into the next person's head. The thing is, we've only been using our word play to convey our own thoughts and opinions, versus tailoring our words to be suitable and attractive to someone else. This is seductive word play.

With this science, it is crucial for you to get outside of your own head and venture into the minds of others. The key is not only the words you use, or the tone of your voice, how it sounds, how its delivered, but more so the ability to adjust your perspective. You must make a radical shift from using words to relay your messages to using them to delight, confuse, and charm others.

I always like to make this analogy: Regular speech is like every day noise that annoys, and people will tune out. Seductive wordplay is like beautiful music—sounds that entice the ears of the listeners.

To make this type of musical language, you have to say things that are pleasing to your target. If they have a lot of issues, you can say things that take them away from all that. Take them on a journey with your witty comments and stories. Entertain them. Make your company a pleasure and they'll love it when you're around. You have to make dialog that is tailored for them, not talk aimed at them. Know the difference.

You can use flattery to a certain extent, but be aware of its limits. Know your mark and what their weaknesses are so that you hit the right places in their vanity. In this way, your words have a positive effect on your target. You're not trying to express your true feelings, but speaking with words that will create the precise emotional state. Learn to aim at a person's insecurities, the areas that need validation. For example, if your target is pretty, don't mention her looks because she hears this all the time. Instead, it will be better to mention some other talent that she has that no one really notices. It's your job to sniff that out. In fact, if the girl is a beauty, you should never compliment her on that. Don't tell her how nice her ass looks in those pants. Instead, tell her that you commend her on the way she responsibly handles her business like a real boss.

One personal mind trick I like to play is to mention you and her inside her kitchen or in her house somewhere. I like to tell them that when I get out I want to cook some food with them. No matter how she reacts, you have no doubt planted an image in her imagination. She has pictured you in her house. Which means she has an image of you in her head, a stain that can't be removed. Do this often with different scenarios. Be descriptive and detailed if she allows it, and more and more your words will be creating images of you and you'll be in her head.

Another angle that you can use in prison is an ancient art form that has long been forsaken and destroyed by our new technological devices: the art of love letters. This is a powerfully effective way to get into your target's head and use poetic words to woo them. Something that no man in her life has ever done. It is wise not to drop a letter on your target until you've had several encounters with her though. I've seen many make the mistake of giving a letter when they first meet the target and end up in the hole for being hasty and stupid, not thinking things through first. Make sure she's okay with it.

Design your letters in way that makes them all about your target and her effect on you. Paint it as if she is all you think of, how no woman has had this effect on you.
Make it as if she's looking into a mirror and seeing herself in a new light, through eyes she's never discovered before. Lay it on thick, but not too thick, as to make her think you're crazy.

Make references to your intentions with her, but be indirect. Tell her about the possibilities of her and you together. Tell her your plans but make them come back to her in some way, merge your wants and hers together. Lead her on a path of potentials that end with her following your lead to your designed "promise land". Everyone loves to hear words of promise and hope, especially naive women. Tell her what she wants to hear, it's as easy as that. Your only task is to find out what she wants to hear. Every woman is a different case.

Don't be surprised if she doesn't write back. That's cool, she's not in position to correspond with a convict back and forth. So just know that she received it and give her more. Your letters can have a poetic flair, but not exactly be poetry. Although that works too, it is not my personal favorite. Design your letters so that they are centered around the target, never speak about yourself.

Make it seem like she is all that you think about. Make it as if she can see herself through your eyes. Use more feelings and emotions in the content versus factual information. Tell her more about your feelings towards her, he effect on you. Make sure you keep your ideas vague and not too detailed, this allows your target to read what she wants to in them, leaving room for her to fantasize. Your goal is to arouse emotion in your target.

THE PULL UP

In this chapter, I want to help equip you with ways you can approach an officer with general lines that can be used as conversation starters. Remember that at the end of the day, they're humans too, and humans are social by nature. One problem that we have is to view them as officers, like robots or something with no feelings. Don't make that mistake, they are very approachable.

One technique is what I call "pecking". This is more so designed for those women who think they're fine and people have placed them on a pedestal. A peck is a way to knock them off of their high horse without arousing resentment or coming off as offensive. It is a slight diss or a shot at their insecurity, but not to the point where they are offended or feel disrespected.

The key to a peck is to have a playful edge to your demeanor, so she knows you're only playing with her and she'll laugh about it herself. A peck is like a light tease. You want to be playful, but not over doing it as to make yourself a clown in her eyes. Here's an example of an effective peck: Say you're talking to her, then you come out suddenly and say, "Damn girl, yo breath smells like tuna and old cheese! What you been eating" This sounds harsh, but it's all about your tone and delivery. If it was in a playful manner, she'll laugh it off and you two will laugh together. You don't want to say it as if you were serious and her breath really is offensive. If done right, this will have a powerful effect.

What this does is knocks her off of her high pedestal, and now she'll want to prove herself to you. In this way, you have reversed the dynamic, you make her want to chase you! You see, everyone compliments her. They say how fine she is, how good her hair looks, whatever. Or they make the mistake of cursing her out, calling her stuck up or telling her bad her attitude is and calling her a bitch. That won't work. She gets that all the time.

In her eyes, everyone thinks that she is perfect though she knows she isn't. But her whole life people have been making her feel like they think she is. This has inflated her ego and raised her to a high throne. But by you pointing out a flaw, even if it doesn't really exist, you have made her self-conscious. Her breath may not smell bad at all but that doesn't matter. Now she has to redeem her perfect image and make you view her as perfect just like everyone else. She'll make it her business to prove her perfection to you. Understand?

You can pretty much mention anything, it doesn't have to be accurate. For instance, say you're talking to her, and you come out of nowhere and say, "Whoa, you blink a lot." and then continue what you were saying. She probably never blinked but just the fact that you mentioned it, she's gonna see that as an imperfection that you noticed. You can be talking, "So I need you to get this form for me from your desk- WHOA, you blink a lot! Anyway, I need this form so I can see medical." You see?

You have to make it like an off-handed comment, not like you're roasting her and shooting shots, it's just that you noticed. It'll seem like an innocent comment. There are many ways to peck. The key is to stab at her insecurities without making it too harsh yet being playful. But do not do this too often. You only need to peck a girl three times at the most, but only two times during one encounter. After you've pecked her enough, you don't have to keep doing it the whole time you deal with her. Pecks are only used in the initial phase. They are used to bring them down to carth a little so once you've knocked them down, then they're good. You don't have to keep doing it. Soon you can actually start building them up again with flattery and compliments.

    Another good opener is to pull up and ask her a question that will start a conversation. One I often use is to tell her that your brother is having a bachelor party, but his fiance doesn't want any strippers there. Ask her opinion on that. If she doesn't elaborate too much on her opinion of this, then you can just ramble on about how you feel about it. Questions like these, there are thousands, they're good ways to open casual conversation with them.

Another tactic is to cut her off in mid-sentence as if what she was saying doesn't matter. Or you can ask her a question and jump to another subject as she's answering. Then later go back to the initial question. This is behavior that most guys don't show to beautiful women, they usually listen intently and hang on their every word, virtually worshipping them. By you doing the opposite and acting differently, they'll label you as different and intriguing.

The main trick when pulling up, and it varies with different officers, is most of them are viewed in prison as dime pieces and they all get placed up high on pedestals, so the trick is to make yourself elevated over them and make them want to chase you. Sometimes you can catch a girl by saying nothing to her at all, ever! She'll wonder why you haven't spoken to her like everyone else has and she may go out of her way to speak to you. Then you can tell her she has a booger in her nose, even if she doesn't. This will surely make her feel insecure and in turn will make her want to straighten her face. She'll want to "put you in your place" so to speak, so she'll go out of her way to make you view her the way everyone else does and kiss her ass.

So, wait for her to push up and try to make small talk with you, nine times out of ten she'll do just that. When she does approach, it'll be good to brush her off again. maybe you can ask her a general question, then when she starts to answer cut her off and change the subject, or even better just walk off on her as if she wasn't saying anything. Acts like these will push her buttons and make her wonder why you're not into her. Now when she tries to talk to you again, which she will, now you can play nice. Indulge in some good conversation with her, maybe even flirt a little, but you should revert back to the cold treatment again at some point. Then go back to talking to her again. All of this activity should go on day to day, each encounter should alternate from hot and cold as you see fit.

What this does is keep her in her place mentally, she'll discover that you are a prize and she has to earn your attention. Never give her too much attention and conversation until she has earned it. This is where most guys go wrong when dealing with women who consider themselves good looking. They give them too much attention at first when she has done nothing to earn it, so she doesn't consider them worthy of her attention. You see? It's a subtle game of value. You have to switch the dynamic. You're the catch and she has to pursue you.

CONCENTRATE ON YOUR FOCUS

One problem that convicts have when it comes to catching is that they spread themselves too thin. They often hit on every woman that they come in contact with. Not only does this make you appear thirsty, but it dissipates your focus which is a powerful tool when used correctly.

In seduction, and life in general, it is of the utmost importance to learn how to focus your energy. This is a scientific fact. If you haven't been introduced to the subtle mental laws that govern not only our lives, but our entire universe, then this may be difficult to wrap your mind around at first. I'll give you a quick overview of what's called the law of attraction. It is a natural law of the universe and is highly effective if used properly.

In general, our minds have a mysterious way of bringing us the physical equivalent of what we think about the most, the predominate thoughts that occupy our minds. If our thoughts and focus is scattered, then we'll rarely achieve anything that we want. If our thoughts are concentrated, focused, then we will be calling on forces that will help us attain the things we focus on.

I don't want to throw you off cause I know how weird this may seem if you haven't heard of this concept, But it is scientifically proven that our lives, and the things that come into them, are in exact proportion to the quality of our thoughts. Ponder this for a moment: if you've ever kept finding yourself in the same predicaments time and time again throughout your life, then this means that you've been thinking the same thoughts over and over which is bringing you the same results. More than likely this is not your first time in prison, why is it that you can't seem to get out of the rut and break this repeated cycle? Simple, you haven't learned how to properly adjust your thinking and thought process.

One proof of this truth is when people, men and women alike, notice that they keep attracting the same type of people in relationships. Women wonder why they always end up with losers or guys who treat them badly. The reason is because they always focus their thoughts on the type of guy that they don't want, instead of focusing on the guy that they do want. They sit around and gossip about their ex-boyfriend, how he behaved, messed up things he's done. This type of thought pattern is lining them up to attract another guy of the same caliber, the same bad characteristics.

How can this be helpful to you in your objectives? Once you have found a target, and you see that she's susceptible to your charm, then focus your thoughts and all your energy on that one target. Think about her as often as you can, even when she's not around. Before you fall asleep at night, ponder over things that you'd like to know about her, how is her personality at home, how does she interact with her kids, what type of clothes does she wear outside of her work uniform.

Picture her. Hold an image of her in your mind, visualize you and her together, talking, maybe getting physical with each other, but most importantly visualize the two of you getting money together since this is the main objective. See this relationship in your mind as if it has already occurred, like it is factual and not just your mind running wild with day dreams. Do this constantly, become so absorbed in your target that she becomes an obsession to you, become totally engulfed in thoughts of her, try to make her all you think about throughout your day.

This may seem odd, but this process is powerful. You'll be surprised how effective it'll be in your endeavors. Find a target and stick with her. Don't even flirt or talk to any other women, she is all that you're concerned with. Not only should you do this with your target, but you should use your mental powers before you even find a target. Spend some time each day, about thirty minutes at least, focusing your mind on seeing yourself getting money in your situation. Know that you've already succeeded. Do this consistently. Make your thoughts intense, bring some emotion into it, get rowed up and make statements to yourself like you mean it! All of this will have a mysteriously powerful effect towards your success.

THE CONCLUSION

At the end of the day, catching an officer or any employee in prison is fairly simple. Though it takes study and patience, its easy once you learn what's going on and how to move. Everyone can catch just by being themselves. They may run into a chick that's feeling them, but I've worked on this project to help you get nearly any officer, or at least more than you would by just being yourself. Seduction in prison is a game of comfort, getting your target comfortable and familiar with you. Most guys fail because they try too hard and come on way too strong way too early.

The main focus of this book is the money and the power, don't lose sight of that. You're working in the realm of manipulation, so you must tread carefully when tampering with the free will of others. Although in the end, you both will come out on top financially, it's still dangerous since you're playing with people's emotions. If you get a girl to fall in love with you, which will happen more often than not, then you must find a way to break the spell you've made, so as to ensure that she's not damaged afterwards. It is rare that you'll find an officer that strictly wants money, though there are some who feel that way, but usually you'll have to play lover boy with most of them.

As you practice your own seductions you may discover new things that I missed, this is only what I've learned from my experience. So, I wouldn't be surprised if there's a lot of other interesting and useful tactics out there that can be used. This is only a general formula and can be tweaked in any way you see fit to suit your personal situation.

In the end I hope you gain much power from the information in this book and I hope you use it for good intentions and to better the financial situation of yourself and your targets. The principles taught have been known to work, but simply reading this book won't help, you must apply the teachings. I hope you turn your prison experience into a profitable one and reach all your goals. Much success to you!

Made in the USA
Columbia, SC
19 May 2020